Bobbie's Story:
A Guide for Foster Parents

Brennan Lynn Mars

CWLA Press • Washington, DC

CWLA Press is an imprint of the Child Welfare League of America. The Child Welfare League of America (CWLA) is a privately supported, nonprofit, membership-based organization committed to preserving, protecting, and promoting the well-being of all children and their families. Believing that children are our most valuable resource, CWLA, through its membership, advocates for high standards, sound public policies, and quality services for children in need and their families.

CHILD WELFARE LEAGUE OF AMERICA, INC.
440 First Street, NW, Third Floor, Washington, DC 20001-2085
E-mail: books@cwla.org

CURRENT PRINTING (last digit)
10 9 8 7 6 5 4 3 2 1

Cover design by Jenny Geanakos
Cover illustration by D. H. Tsai

Printed in the United States of America

ISBN # 0–87868-701-7

Library of Congress Cataloging-in-Publication Data
Mars, Brennan Lynn.
Bobbie's story : a guide for foster parents / Brennan Lynn Mars : illustrations by D.H. Tsai.
p. cm.
To be used in conjunction with: Bobbie's story : a feelings workbook.
ISBN 0-87868-701-7
1. Child sexual abuse--Psychological aspects. 2. Sexually abused children--Psychology. 3. Foster children--Psychology. 4. Foster home care. I. Title.
HV6570.M37 1998 98-24249
618.92'85836--dc221

To Bela, with love.

Contents

Professional Disclaimer

Due to the subject matter of *Bobbie's Story*, the author recommends that her materials not be used without the guidance of a treatment professional. Should you obtain a copy of the workbook and/or foster parent guide, please consult your child's social worker or therapist to help you in using the workbook.

Preface

An increasing number of children are being referred to foster care after being identified as sexually abused—and child sexual abuse is a difficult issue for us to understand. To most of us, the sexual molestation of a child is frightening and disgusting. In addition, the association of children and sexuality stirs up uncomfortable feelings. We find ourselves questioning our own sexual feelings. Often we experience anger at the perpetrator. Sometimes we wonder if the child was at fault by seducing the adult. Sometimes we relive feelings about sexual experiences in our own childhood.

These uncomfortable feelings may cause us to think that if we just don't think about "it," or talk about "it," the child will forget about "it." Unfortunately, pretending that there is no problem only makes the problem worse. The thoughts and memories of having been abused remain with children for many years, often into their own adulthood. It is comforting for abused children to know that we understand what the child has gone through.

It is important for you as a foster parent to understand that you are not alone in feeling uncomfortable about caring for a sexually abused child. Being aware of these feelings and talking about them with your partners, with other foster parents, and with helping professionals, however, may lessen the anxiety.

If you can acknowledge the uncomfortable nature of sexual abuse, you will be better able to help your foster child. Children who have been sexually abused need to understand what happened to them, that it was not their fault, and they need to know how to prevent being sexually abused again. As foster parents, you may find these helpful suggestions about how to set limits and provide support and encouragement to sexually abused children in your care to be useful. The importance of using treatment professionals for support and guidance in helping the sexually abused child, however, can not be overemphasized.

Introduction

Bobbie's Story: A Feelings Workbook and *Bobbie's Story: A Guide for Foster Parents* have been designed with two goals. First, the *Workbook* may encourage an environment in which the foster child may begin to feel comfortable discussing sexual abuse issues with you. (Many children may never feel comfortable discussing their abuse experience with you and should not be forced to do so. Introducing an atmosphere in which the child may begin to feel comfortable talking about his or her abuse experience, however, may be helpful.) The *Guide* provides you with information about the nature of the sexual abuse experience, resulting behavior and feelings, and suggestions for handling this behavior.

The *Workbook* is about a young child (Bobbie) living in foster care, who was sexually abused before moving into the foster home. The *Workbook* has been developed for use with male and female children ages 5-10. You and the child should read the *Workbook* together.

The *Guide* has been designed to help you care for sexually abused children and is divided into five sections: self-blame (and how others may view sexual abuse), betrayal, powerlessness, adjusting to new rules, and empowering the sexually abused child. These sections correspond to the colored pages in the *Workbook*. (Colors and page numbers are indicated in the text.)

Some children may not benefit from the interactive nature of the *Workbook* because of the degree of anxiety about their experience and/or their inability to attend to the *Workbook*. For children who wish to remain silent about their experiences, you may read the *Workbook* to them and disregard the open-ended questions.

In either situation, you can use the *Guide* and the *Workbook* together to help both the child who chooses to be a silent participant and the child who chooses to be an active participant understand several things:

- Sexual abuse does happen to other children too,
- The child is not alone,
- The sexual abuse is not the child's fault,
- The child is having normal feelings,
- There are ways that the child can feel more in charge of what happens and ways to prevent being abused in the future, and
- There are rules and boundaries that are associated with healthy relationships with adults.

Remember, children who have been sexually abused will need the guidance of treatment professionals in many developmental stages throughout their lives to become healthy, functioning adults. The help needed will vary, depending on the severity and nature of the child's abuse experience.

Self-Blame

Many child victims of sexual abuse feel as if they are responsible for that abuse, especially when they realize how other people view sexual activity between children and adults. In addition, many children do not realize that such activity is wrong until they see the negative reactions of others who find out about the abuse. Those responses, in turn, may cause the child to feel guilty or ashamed.

Feelings Workbook: pp. 8-9 (yellow)

Children who have been sexually abused often feel responsible for the disruption that occurs in their family after the sexual abuse is disclosed. The guilt these children feel after they have disclosed is intensified if family members do not believe the child, or if they blame the child for the sexual activity.

Suggestions for Foster Parents

- Consistently explain and reassure the child that she is not to blame for the sexual activity.
- Explain to the child that she was placed in foster care because she was not safe in her family.

Feelings Workbook: pp. 10-13 (yellow)

Often children who have been sexually abused feel responsible for not ending the abuse sooner. Once they understand that the sexual abuse was wrong, children may begin to blame themselves for playing sexual games and even for enjoying the sexual games with the abuser. In fact, many children may have enjoyed the experience, the rewards, the closeness, and attention they got from the trusted figure. When they realize that the sexual activity was wrong, they may feel guilty that they enjoyed the experience.

It may be difficult for many foster parents, and adults in general, to accept that a child may enjoy some aspects of sexual abuse. Many presume, incorrectly, that children are not capable of having sexual feelings. It is important for you to recognize your own discomfort about thinking of children as sexual beings, so that the child does not feel more dirty or ashamed as a result of your reactions.

Suggestions for Foster Parents

- Allow the child to express whatever feeling he has without responding negatively; that reaction may add to the child's guilty feelings.
- Communicate to the child that it is natural to enjoy the attention and closeness that he felt with the abuser, but that there are other ways to be close to an adult that do not involve sexual activity.

Feelings Workbook: pp. 14-15 (yellow)

Many children who have been sexually abused may feel responsible for not being able to stop or avoid their abuser. They may feel that they could have told sooner, or run away from home, or predicted when the abuse was more likely to occur (i.e., after school) and, instead of going home, gone to a friend's house.

Suggestions for Foster Parents

- Communicate to the child that it is not her fault.
- Communicate to the child that it would have been difficult to avoid her abuser, and that it is not her responsibility to have to predict the abuse or avoid it by going to a friend's house or staying away from home.

Feelings Workbook: pp. 16-17 (yellow)

Finally, many children may feel different, dirty, and ashamed after being sexually abused. These children may feel that other people will be able to tell what happened to them, and that they won't be liked as a result.

Suggestions for Foster Parents

- Reassure the child that she is not "dirty."
- Show the child her value by helping her identify her unique talents and/or skills; help her recognize and appreciate her abilities.
- Reassure the child that others cannot know about what happened to her unless they are told.

Betrayal

Children may feel betrayed when they realize that someone they depended on caused them harm. Children may feel betrayed because a trusted family member was unable or unwilling to protect or believe them. Children who are disbelieved or blamed will undoubtedly experience a greater sense of betrayal. Children who have been betrayed will experience feelings of anger, sadness, confusion, and fear.

ANGER
Feelings Workbook: pp. 18-19 (blue)

Many children who have been sexually abused will experience extreme anger that stems from feelings of betrayal. They may feel angry at family, other adults, and society for allowing the abuse to occur. Furthermore, they may be angry for being removed from their family. Children may express anger about telling their story about the sexual abuse over and over to case workers, doctors, lawyers, judges, and to foster parents. They may be unwilling to talk about the abuse experience for several reasons:

- Embarrassment;
- Feelings of responsibility for the breakup of family, negative reactions from adults and family members, incarceration of the abuser, etc.;
- The desire to protect the perpetrator; and
- Feelings of being overwhelmed with sadness, fear, betrayal, and confusion.

Angry reactions might be directed outward or inward. Outward anger may be seen as rebellion and negative or destructive behaviors. Inward anger, when children believe they are "bad," may be more damaging and may lead to depression and despair.

Suggestions for Foster Parents

- Explain to the child that it is all right to be angry. Allow the child to vent anger in an appropriate manner.
- Make sure that the rules about appropriate expressions of anger are clear (i.e., it is OK to yell, scream, and hit a pillow, but not OK to hit a person).
- While you should never force a child to talk about his experiences, it may be helpful to let him know that you are there to listen and help if he needs you or wants to talk.
- You might help the child gradually gain control over unacceptable outbursts of anger with the following steps:
  - Plan and provide positive consequences for appropriate behavior and negative consequences for inappropriate behavior.
  - Use clear and specific consequences that fit the approved or unapproved behavior.
  - Be consistent with consequences across settings, over time, and between parents.
  - Plan incentives that produce positive behavior before punishing negative behavior. (Punishment is not effective for reducing negative behavior without a program for rewarding appropriate alternative behaviors.)
  - Recognize, then anticipate, the foster child's misbehavior and develop methods that reduce the probability of such misbehavior.

Ask your case worker/child therapist for further clarification of these five steps.

Feelings Workbook: pp. 20-21

These two pages are designed to stimulate discussion between the foster parent and child. Pencils, crayons, and extra sheets of paper will enhance the interactive experience. Each child should be encouraged to proceed at her own pace. Some questions may be too difficult to address at first and may be reviewed later, when you have established a better relationship with the child. Again, however, many children may never feel comfortable revealing their feelings to their foster parents. Thus, children may benefit from reading or listening to the story without answering or discussing their own experience until they feel more comfortable doing so. Knowing that you are interested in discussing these issues, however, may facilitate children's comfort level in beginning to relay their experience.

SADNESS
Feelings Workbook: pp. 22-23 (blue)

Sadness or grief reactions may occur over the betrayal and loss of trusted figures. The physical separation that occurs when the child is removed from his home, regardless of the severity of the abuse, will also be painful.

Some children may first respond to the new foster home with shock. A child may behave almost perfectly at first, but if he is not returned to his biological family (despite all efforts), he may show feelings of anger (as discussed above), followed by grief and feelings of despair. (See the section on anger, page 7.)

Suggestions for Foster Parents

- Encourage children to talk about good memories along with the bad memories of the abuse and abuser.
- Refrain from taking the position that the child's birth parents are "bad."
- Listen to and support the expression of the child's feelings.
- Use thoughtful language to explain the reason for the child's removal from home, such as, "Mommy

and Daddy are unable to keep you safe right now, and Mommy and Daddy need help to learn how to keep you safe."

Feelings Workbook: pp. 24-25

See directions for Workbook pages 20-21, on page 8 in this Guide.

CONFUSION
Feelings Workbook: pp. 26-27 (blue)

An abused child may be confused about whom to trust, because the adults whom she previously trusted and loved betrayed her (i.e., the abuser betrayed the child through the abuse, the other adults betrayed the child by not protecting her from the abuser). Even though the child feels betrayed and mistrustful, however, she may still love these adults. Thus, there may be additional confusion about how she may feel anger, betrayal, and resentment on the one hand, and love for these same adults on the other.

Additionally, children that have been abused may feel relieved to be living with and protected by foster parents, but angry not to be with their birth parents. These confusing feelings toward foster parents and birth parents will often produce feelings of guilt and the belief that it is "bad" to have such feelings.

Children who have been abused are often confused when people act pleasantly to them, especially if they think of themselves as "bad." The child might think, "Who would be nice to me? I don't deserve for someone to be nice to me." An abused child might suspect that a nice person wants something in return, because she might have learned that niceness doesn't come without a cost. Finally, the foster child may become confused when he receives conflicting messages from his birth parents, social workers, and foster parents about why he is in foster care.

Suggestions for Foster Parents

- Recognize that the child who has been abused may have confused feelings about the foster parents, as well as about birth parents. Once foster parents recognize that these feelings exist, they can
  - provide a predictable and consistent environment that may enable the child to express feelings of confusion,
  - be patient while the child becomes accustomed to her new environment, and
  - allow enough time to experience some pleasant and consistent relationships.
- Provide factual information to the child about reasons for placement, etc., and encourage the child to express her beliefs about the reason for placement, so that she will not be so confused. Remember, however, that even the truth may not enhance the child's ability to deal with the reality of her situation.

Feelings Workbook: pp. 28-29

See directions for Workbook pages 20-21, on page 8 in this Guide.

FEAR/SCARY FEELINGS
Feelings Workbook: pp. 30-31 (blue)

Fear has been a constant experience of child victims of sexual abuse. They may fear the consequences of the sexual activity (i.e., being physically damaged). They may also fear what people would think about them or what would happen if they told (i.e., physical abuse, family breakup, blame for sexual activity, etc.). Finally, they may also fear the next abusive incident.

Children who have been abused may bring fear, an impaired ability to trust, and experiences of an unpredictable environment in which expression of anger or fear were not tolerated with them to their new foster home. Because of these experiences, the foster child is likely to fear foster parents and may initially expect them to be as unpredictable as previous adult models. Often, the fears that abused children have will be shown in the form of nightmares and sleep disturbances, withdrawal or aggression, eating disorders, and phobias.

Suggestions for Foster Parents

- Encourage (but never force) foster children to talk about their fears related to the sexual abuse, fears about what will happen to them and their natural parents, fears about what others think about them, and fears associated with adjusting to a new environment.
- Be patient, because fears may resurface again and again, or may be triggered by other scary events in the child's life, even when you think that the child has worked through all her fears.

Feelings Workbook: pp. 32-33

See directions for Workbook pages 20-21, on page 8 in this Guide.

Powerlessness/ Helplessness

Powerlessness begins when a child's territory and body space are repeatedly invaded against her will. Powerlessness increases when children are continuously fearful, when they are unable to make other adults believe what is happening, or when they realize that being dependent on the abuser has trapped them in the abusive situation. Powerlessness will also increase when force and threats are used to ensure that the child does not tell on the abuser and when the child is removed from her birth parents against her will.

Feelings Workbook: pp. 34-35 (red)

Child sexual abuse involves a violation of the child's body, privacy, and sense of control. The child may have continuously felt trapped by threats of harm or fear of the consequences of disclosing to someone. These experiences teach the child that she has no control over her life, that there is no freedom to make choices, and that giving up is the only solution in most situations.

Additionally, the child's removal from home into foster care may be just another experience that verifies for the child that he has no control over what happens to him. This sense of powerlessness or helplessness may clearly lead to a low self-image that may make it difficult for the child to make friends, assert his needs, take risks, and learn in school.

Feelings of powerlessness in children may be exhibited through temper tantrums, losing patience easily, fights at school, depression or withdrawal, a need for control over small choices (i.e., choice of clothes, bedtime, etc.), or a constant need to please.

Suggestions for Foster Parents

- Give foster children opportunities to make choices and be responsible for their own actions without fearing punishment.
- Encourage extracurricular activities to instill a sense of accomplishment.
- Encourage learning by providing support and letting the child know that it is all right to make mistakes. (A nurturing environment may allow the child to gain the confidence necessary to risk failure and to learn to do her best to succeed.)
- Model ways that children might assert their rights. Also, assert the rights of the child on her behalf until she is ready to speak for herself.

Adjusting to New Rules

Feelings Workbook: pp. 36-43 (green)

Children who have been sexually abused are often confused by the new rules of the foster family. For example, allowing others to have privacy, understanding how to give and receive appropriate affection from adults and children, or knocking before entering someone's bedroom or the bathroom may be new experiences.

Children who have been sexually abused also have difficulty giving up old roles. Often these children assume more adultlike roles in their family. For example, in a father-daughter incest case, the daughter may take over the role of spouse, parent to other siblings, and household caretaker.

The sexual behavior exhibited by children that have been sexually abused is often the most difficult to accept by foster parents.

Suggestions for Foster Parents

- Communicate and model clear rules of appropriate adult/child relationships for the child.
  - Children who have been sexually abused should not be allowed to get into the foster parent bed.
  - No one touches another person without asking that person's permission.
  - Touching games, such as tickling and wrestling, should be prohibited.
  - All individuals (old enough to care for themselves) should have privacy in bathing, dressing, and toileting.
  - No one should go outside the bathroom or bedroom without clothing.
  - Some behaviors are appropriate in private but not in public (i.e., masturbation).

- Allow the child who has assumed adultlike responsibilities to do more age appropriate chores in the foster home. Such a child should be encouraged to assume a more childlike role and to act as a child.
- Help the child to develop a healthy understanding of sexual relations between adults by explaining that there are some things that grown-ups do that children don't do (e.g., drive cars, work at jobs, drink alcohol, and stay up late). Explain that the abuser did things that were not OK, because it is illegal to do such adult things with children. It may be helpful to explain further that some of the things that the child experienced are things that grown-ups who love each other do together. (Obviously, this would not be said to a child that had been violently molested.) The foster parent can say to the child that the abuser has a problem because he does sexual things with children instead of grown-ups.
- Be careful not to make negative statements about the abuser, since the child may have positive feelings about him/her. It was the abuser's behavior that was negative.

Empowering the Sexually Abused Child

Feelings Workbook: pp. 44-49 (orange)

As mentioned previously in this guide, sexual abuse may leave the child with a sense of helplessness. These feelings of having no control in her life will leave her in danger of further victimization. Thus, it is important to empower the child with the knowledge that she does have some control and that she can do things to try to avoid being abused again.

This must be done in a tone that does not make the child feel responsible for the abuse that has already occurred (i.e., "It is not your fault that Sam did those things to you. There was no way for you to know how to stop him or prevent him from doing those things, but there are some things that you can learn now to try to protect yourself from being abused again.").

Suggestions for Foster Parents

- Teach the child about the difference between good touches and bad touches. Help the child understand what parts of his body are private and belong only to him.
- Give children who have been sexually abused permission to say no to adults, to run away from people who scare them, and encourage children to ask for help.
- Over time, model behavior that helps the child understand that most adults are not like the abuser and will help her if she is in danger.

Final Note to Foster Parents

It is my hope that this guide provides you with useful information about children who have been sexually victimized. The experience of caring for a child who has been sexually abused can be a challenge that will require the knowledge and skills of treatment professionals. I urge you to stay in contact with these professionals for support and guidance with respect to managing the child's behavior, providing the best possible care for the child, and providing a sounding board for you in managing the questions and concerns that will arise.

About the Author

Brennan Lynn Mars, Psy.D., conducts family therapy, play therapy, couples and marital therapy, and parenting skills training; provides crisis intervention; and administers psychodiagnostic tests to children at the Julia Ann Singer Center in Los Angeles, California. She received her doctorate in Clinical Psychology with an individual/family/child proficiency from the California School of Professional Psychology in Los Angeles.

About *Bobbie's Story . . .*

by
Brennan Lynn Mars

Bobbie's Story: A Feelings Workbook tells the story of a young child who was sexually abused and is now living with foster parents. It is designed to be read together by the child and foster parent, once foster parents have received appropriate guidance and training.

Bobbie's Story: A Guide for Foster Parents (sold separately) provides foster parents with information about the sexual abuse of children, resulting behavior and feelings, and suggestions for working with abused children as they deal with their experiences. The *Guide* is divided into sections that correspond with pages in the *Workbook*: self-blame (and how others view sexual abuse), betrayal, powerlessness, adjusting to new rules, and empowering the sexually abused child.

To order *Bobbie's Story: A Feelings Workbook*

1999/0-87868-735-1	Stock #7351	$5.95

To order additional copies of *Bobbie's Story: A Guide for Foster Parents*

1999/0-87868-701-7	Stock #7017	$12.95

Write:	CWLA P.O. Box 2019 Annapolis Junction, MD 20701-2019	Call:	800/407-6273 301/617-7825
E-mail:	cwla@pmds.com	Fax:	301/206-9789

Bulk discount policy (not for resale): 10-49 copies 10%, 50-99 copies 20%, 100 or more copies 40%. Canadian and foreign orders must be prepaid in U.S. funds. MasterCard/Visa accepted.